Copyright © 2020

Alaina Clark Tyson

All rights reserved. No part of this publication may be reproduced, stored in a retrieval system or transmitted in any way by any means, electronic, mechanical, photocopy, recording or otherwise without the prior permission of the author except as provided by USA copyright law.

BEAR WITH US

BOOK 1

BY
ALAINA CLARK TYSON

The day started out like any other.
I ate some food, took a walk and wrestled with my brother.

Life was good there, but I wanted to know more about life in other places.

So, I called for my crew, set out on a walk and even had some races.

It was just then I learned so very much and wished that I had stayed.

But instead I chose to get my friends involved - to leave our home and play.

I took a tumble down a little hill and landed with a thud.

My friends were gone, I was all alone in the nasty, sticky mud.

I was frightened, tear drops formed in my eyes, the trees were crying too.

Their tears got me soaking wet, but I knew just what to do.

Mom taught me to stay cool and dry and always to be brave.

So, I looked around and found it then - a perfect place - my cave!

It was a little higher than my cave back with my crew.

But it was warmer and quieter than any cave I ever knew.

My cave got dark so very fast and from the forest not a peep.

I tried to fight the urge, but exhaustion won, and I quickly fell asleep.

I woke to light of day and sounds I had never heard.

They weren't sounds my friends would make or even caws of birds.

Then a boom and a shake of my cave but I stayed safely inside.

I hunkered down, stayed nice and low, this was my place to hide.

Another nap, more time had passed and hungry I was growing.

Darkness fell again outside my cave and I pressed something without knowing.

I was more scared than ever before of that sound that came to get me.

I searched everywhere for a way out - I wanted to be free!

But that loud sound continued as I tried to leave my place.

I thought I had picked the best cave but that was clearly not the case.

I was stuck inside my cave with tears of fury in eyes and ears.

I called for my family and my friends but not a one was near.

So, I did what all good bears would do, and I used my strength and nails.

Piercing booms never stopped while I tried to get out, but I couldn't - I failed.

Just then a light in my cave and the noises - they got worse.

What was going on? What could this be? I feel like I've been cursed!

I saw creatures trying to get to me and the blaring booms kept going.

One of them came close to me, opened my cave as sounds kept growing.

It was then I saw I had an out - a way to see my mama bear.

So, I jumped right down out of my cave into the cool night's autumn air.

I saw the hill from which I fell and up it I climbed so fast.

I found my mom and she didn't believe my story of the day's past.

But that's ok - I'm not upset - I'm just glad I'm out and great.

I'm so happy I got out of that little cave and that creature opened my gate!

BEAR WITH US

BOOK 2

BY

ALAINA CLARK TYSON

We had to leave - the hurricane was near.
To safety we must go.

In the mountains we'd be safe from harm!
Of that I surely know.

It was a long ride, but we had fun playing games and singing songs.

Traffic slowed us quite a bit - the trip was extra long.

We made it to the cabin and saw it was atop a huge, steep hill.

A perfect place for our evacuation and not so full of frill.

We unpacked, cleared the car and unloaded all our gear.

The cabin was great, up on a hill with mountains so very near.

We played some ball, relaxed and read and enjoyed the mountain air.

But wait - the ranger on our hike said, "Be careful and watch out for bear".

I was doubtful we'd see one. I was sure they'd hide in caves with all their friends.

So, I thought we'd enjoy our mountain home before our vacation ends.

The next full day was lots of fun. Played some ball and it was great.

An evening meal of shrimp and grits, showers, books - it was getting late.

Then it was time to sleep again. Kids snuggled in their beds.

They said their prayers, hugged and kissed and laid down their little heads.

I was thankful for more days in that beautiful mountain place.

It felt so relaxing to be there and out of the busy city pace.

I knew we were up there all alone, but I swear I heard some honking.

So, I jumped up, right out of bed, but my head it went a bonking!

I grabbed my bathrobe and my light and ran right up to the door.

I looked outside to darkness, heard our car horn honking and then a **ROAR**.

On turned the light and I was shocked to see a **BEAR** in the driver's seat!

Honking the horn and roaring to get out.
I'm sure he needed to eat!

I didn't want to be his meal so careful I had to stay.

I just ran, opened the front door and then scrambled to get away.

And that's just how it went. Then I ran back in the cabin.

That bear climbed right down out of the seat - felt like a dream that I was having.

But it was real and so was he and I think he bowed to thank me.

Then he turned slowly and climbed that little hill, so happy to finally flee.

And I went to my car and saw it all then - there was nothing left in there!

I cannot believe my car was demolished by a big, huge, black bear!

I must have accidentally trapped him while I unloaded all the gear.

But I'm so glad we got to see this amazing sight at our cabin up there.

So, next time you're in that neck of the woods say hi to our big, black bear.

But, best way to see him is from this little book. It's safer than getting near.

The story you just read is true. Well, the first book from the bear's perspective is what I THINK the bear was thinking when he decided to get into our car. But all the rest really is TRUE. After evacuating our home due to an impending hurricane, my family and I drove from Charleston, South Carolina to the mountains of Sevierville, Tennessee. We got there in the evening as the sun was going down. Poppy unloaded the car and kept the tailgate open to make the trips back and forth to the car easier. We didn't know it then because it was dark, and he was silent, but the bear was already in the car when Poppy went out to close the back of the car. The next day we played football and walked by the car dozens of times. We never noticed he was in there which is why I assumed he was hunkered down and probably sleeping. The bear was in the car for 28 hours! The cabin we rented was literally on top of the steepest hill we had ever seen. So, when we heard the car horn honking, we knew something strange was happening. The kids were fast asleep. Mom, Poppy and I had to decide who was going to let the bear out of the car and our brave Poppy was up for the challenge. After Poppy opened the car door the bear climbed out so slowly, looked like he bowed to thank us and then he scurried up the same hill he slid down. Due to all of the damage the bear caused to the car it never worked again and had to be towed down from that very steep hill. That was definitely a once in a lifetime story for all of us. Thank you for reading our story - Alaina

alainatyson.com

www.ingramcontent.com/pod-product-compliance
Lightning Source LLC
Chambersburg PA
CBHW061754290426
44108CB00029B/2988